The Victorian Cat

THE VICTORIAN CAT

A Classic Collection for Cat Lovers

Edited by
STED MAYS

WINGS BOOKS
New York / Avenel, New Jersey

FOR

Charles Björklund, whose unstinting encouragement
and support helped to make this volume possible

AND FOR

Pat Sommers, beloved sister and friend, who introduced
the editor and designer of this book to one another

Copyright ©1995 by Sted Mays
All rights reserved.

This edition is published by Wings Books,
distributed by Random House Value Publishing, Inc.,
40 Engelhard Avenue, Avenel, New Jersey 07001,
by arrangement with the author.

Random House

New York • Toronto • London • Sydney • Auckland

Printed and bound in Mexico

Library of Congress Cataloging-in-Publication Data

The Victorian cat : a classic collection for cat lovers / edited by Sted Mays

p.cm.

ISBN 0-517-14727-0

1. Cats--Literary collections. I. Mays, Sted

PN6071.C3V53   1995

808.88'2--dc20

95-20824

CIP

8 7 6 5 4 3 2 1

CONTENTS

Preface *vi*

1

The Victorian Cat in Kittenhood *1*

2

The Victorian Cat as a Symbol
of Domestic Bliss *13*

3

The Victorian Cat as Predator *23*

4

The Victorian Cat as Comedian *29*

5

The Victorian Cat as
Independent Philosopher *39*

6

The Victorian Cat as the
Embodiment of Fear *45*

7

The Victorian Cat Among
the Angels *53*

PREFACE

$\mathcal{T}$HIS BOOK is a gathering of passages from texts produced during and around the time of Victoria's reign on the throne of England, a reign that lasted from 1837 to 1901. I have endeavored to provide the reader with a representative sampling of the most entertaining selections (some adapted especially for this volume) from the vast literary and visual resources of the period. Those who are approaching these resources for the first time, as well as those who are returning to these much-loved texts for repeat visits, will find this collection organized around the various themes listed in the preceding table of contents.

Clearly, the diversity of thematic uses to which the Victorian cat was put is a testament to the creativity and imaginative dexterity of the era. Contained in the following chapters are the works of great authors and lesser talents who were inspired by the feline mania that swept the world in the nineteenth century.

Joan Sommers, a considerable talent in her own right, has designed this collection with sensitivity to the visual spirit of Victorian elegance rather than Victorian kitsch. It is my hope that you will come away from her work as delighted and refreshed as I was. Now pour yourself a cup of tea, sit back, and let your troubles fade from memory while the genius of the Victorian cat beguiles you.

STED MAYS

The Victorian Cat in Kittenhood

"Kittens, you are very little,
And your kitten bones are brittle,
If you'd grow to cats respected,
See your play be not neglected."

IN THE HAY-LOFT

Up in the hay-loft—kitten and I!
With a window open to the sky,
Curtained with boughs of the chestnut trees
That toss and sway in the cool west breeze.

The dome of the sky with a cloud is lined,
And the rain comes down when it has a mind,
Pelting the leaves of the chestnut tree;
Never the rain can touch kitten and me.

Up in the hay-loft—kitten and I!
The hay behind us is mountain high;
The beams across are dusty enough;
Darkness broods in the peak of the roof.

2

In pearly lines the daylight falls
Through the chinks of the boarded walls;
The air is fragrant with clover dried,
Brake and daisies and things beside.

Queer little spiders drop down from on high;
Softly we welcome them—kitten and I!
Swallows chirp in a lazy strain
Between the showers of the summer rain.

Let the rain come down from the clouded sky,
We're quiet and cozy—kitten and I!
We muse and purr and think out a rhyme,
And never know what has become of time.

People down there in the world below,
They toil and moil and get dinner and sew;
Up in the hay we lazily lie;
We have no troubles—kitten and I!

Kitten purrs and stretches and winks,
She doesn't speak, but I know what she thinks;
    Never a king had a throne so high,
Never a bird had a cozier nest;
There is much that is good, but we have the best—
    Kitten, kitten and I!

—HELEN THAYER HUTCHESON

3

KITTY AT SCHOOL

Come, kitty dear, I'll tell you what
　　　We'll do this rainy day;
Just you and I, all by ourselves,
　　　At keeping school, will play.

The teacher, kitty, I will be;
　　　And you shall be the class;
And you must close attention give,
　　　If you expect to pass.

Now, kitty, "C-A-T" spells cat.
　　　Stop playing with your tail!
You are so heedless, I am sure
　　　In spelling you will fail.

"C-A" oh, kitty! do sit still!
　　　You must not chase that fly!
You'll never learn a single word,
　　　You do not even try.

I'll tell you what my teacher says
　　　To me most ev'ry day—
She says that girls can never learn
　　　While they are full of play.

So try again—another word;
    "L-A-C-E" spells "lace."
Why, kitty, it is not polite
    In school to wash your face!

You are a naughty, naughty puss,
    And keep you in I should;
But, then, I love you, dear, so much
    I don't see how I could!

O, see! the sun shines bright again!
    We'll run outdoors and play;
We'll leave our school and lessons for
    Another rainy day.

—KATE ULMER

DOCTOR TOM MEW

This is the Schoolmaster, Doctor Tom Mew,
Who teaches young kittens, and birches them, too;
When he cries "Silence!", each pupil turns pale,
And trembles right down to the tip of his tail.

—Anonymous

THE DEMON KITTENS

I've two pretty little kittens—
    one is brown and one is gray—
You should see the comic antics that
    the little demons play.
You would roll about with laughter
    and I fancy shed a tear,
If you watched them play at leap-frog
    on my crowded chiffonier.

All the china does a-tremble—
    it anticipates its doom—
When those kittens do a-scamper
    round and round my dining-room.
You can almost hear the sideboard
    give a moan and cry "Alas!"
When the leader goes a cropper
    and brings down a row of glass.

Then to see them climb the curtains
        is enough to kill a saint;
Little rips they are for certain—
        those they manufacture ain't;
For the lace is all in tatters,
        and they poke their little heads
Through the hangings at the window,
        which their claws reduce to shreds.

When the poet's pains are on me,
        and my brain is on the rack,
They've a habit of a-lighting
        with a jump upon my back.
Playing with pens and paper
        is a thing at which I wink,
But they might abstain from fishing
        with their fore-paws in the ink.

They have pulled out all the stuffing
        from my best morocco suite,
All my carpets have been ruined
        by their scratching little feet;
But I do not mind the damage,
        though it grieves my better-half,
For the world has made me wretched,
        and my kittens make me laugh.

—ANONYMOUS

MISTRESS KITTY

"Mistress Kitty, from the city,
How do your kittens grow?
        With eyes so bright,
        And fur so white,
And teeth a shining row?"

"My kittens white, my heart's delight,
Their fur is just like snow;
        They play and fight
        From morn till night,
And *that's* the way they grow."

—ANONYMOUS

KITTEN GOSSIP

"Kitten, kitten, two months old,
    Woolly snowball lying snug,
Curl'd up in the warmest fold
    Of the warm hearthrug,
Turn your drowsy head this way.
What is life? O kitten, say!"

"Life!" said the kitten, winking her eyes
And twitching her tail, in a droll surprise—
"Life?—O! it's racing over the floor,
Out at the window and in at the door;
Now on the chair-back, now on the table,
'Mid balls of cotton and skeins of silk,
And crumbs of sugar and jugs of milk,
All so cozy and comfortable.
It's patting the little dog's ears, and leaping
Round him and over him while he's sleeping,
Waking him up in a sore affright,
Then off and away, like a flash of light,
Scouring and scampering out of sight.
Life? O! it's rolling over and over
On the summer-green turf and budding clover,

Chasing the shadows, as fast as they run,
Down the garden paths, in the mid-day sun,
Prancing and gambolling, brave and bold,
Climbing the tree-stems, scratching the mould—
That's life!" said the kitten two months old.

"Kitten, kitten, come sit on my knee,
And lithe and listen, kitten, to me!
One by one, one by one,
The sly, swift shadows sweep over the sun—
Daylight dieth, and—kittenhood's done.
And, kitten, O! the rain and the wind!
For cathood cometh, with careful mind,
And grave cat-duties follow behind."

—THOMAS WESTWOOD

The Victorian Cat as a Symbol of Domestic Bliss

"A cat is the joy of the household."

TO A CAT

Stately, kindly, lordly friend,
    Condescend
Here to sit by me, and turn
Glorious eyes that smile and burn,
Golden eyes, love's lustrous meed,
On the golden page I read.

All your wondrous wealth of hair,
    Dark and fair,
Silken-shaggy, soft and bright
As the clouds and beams of night,
Pays my reverent hand's caress
Back with friendlier gentleness.

Dogs may fawn on all and some,
    As they come;
You, a friend of loftier mind,
Answer friends alone in kind;
Just your foot upon my hand
Softly bids it understand.

—ALGERNON CHARLES SWINBURNE

DON PIERROT DE NAVARRE

*P*IERROT received his name in kittenhood, on account of his immaculate whiteness. His title was added later, and was a tribute to his size and majesty of demeanor. He had a charming disposition, and shared our family life with an intimacy which is possible only to cats who are treated with gentleness and consideration. Sitting close to the fire, he seemed always interested in the conversation, and now and then, as he looked from one speaker to another, he would give a little protesting mew, as though in remonstrance to some opinion which he could not bring himself to share. He adored books, and whenever he found one open on the table, he would sit down by it, look attentively at the printed page, turn over a leaf or two, and finally fall asleep, for all the world as if he had been trying to read a modern novel. As soon as he saw me sit down to write, he would jump on my desk, and watch the crooked and fantastic figures which my pen scattered over the paper, turning his head every time I began a fresh line. Sometimes it occurred to him to take a part in my work, and then he would make little clutches at my pen, with the evident design of writing a page or so; for I more than half suspect him of composing a volume of memoirs, scribbling feverishly at night in some remote gutter by the light of his own gleaming eyes. Alas, that such compositions should have been lost forever!

It is no easy task to win the friendship of a cat. He is a philosopher, sedate, tranquil, a creature of habit, a lover of decency and order. He does not bestow his regard lightly, and, though he may consent to be your companion, he will never be your slave. Even in his most affectionate moods he preserves his freedom, and refuses a servile obedience. But once gain his absolute confidence, and he is a friend for life. He shares your hours of work, of solitude, of melancholy. He spends whole evenings on your knee, purring and dozing, content with your silence, and spurning for your sake the society of his kind. In vain loud miaulings from the neighboring roof summon him to those choice entertainments where red herrings take the place of tea. He pays no heed, and cannot be tempted from your side. If you put him down, he leaps back again, mewing a gentle protest. From time to time he looks into your face with eyes so human, so full of understanding and regard, that you are smitten by fear. Can it be possible that there is no thought behind that absorbed and mysterious scrutiny?—THEOPHILE GAUTIER

THE COMPANIONABLE CAT

My cat in winter time usually sleeps upon my dog, who submits in patience; and I have often found her on horseback in the stable, not from any taste for equestrianism, but simply because a horse-cloth is a perpetual warmer when there is a living horse beneath it. She loves the dog and horse with the tender regard we have for foot-warmers and railway rugs

18

during a journey in the depth of winter; nor have I ever been able to detect in her any worthier sentiment towards her master. Yet of all animals that we can have in a room with us, the cat is the least disquieting. Her presence is soothing to a student, as the presence of a quiet nurse is soothing to an invalid. It is agreeable to feel that you are not absolutely alone, and it seems to you, when you are at work, as if the cat took care that all her movements should be noiseless, purely out of consideration for your comfort. Then, if you have time to caress her, you know that she will purr a response, and why inquire too closely into the sincerity of her affection?—PHILIP GILBERT HAMERTON

FIRELIGHT

Musing, I sit on my cushioned settle,
    Facing the firelight's fitful shine;
Sings on the hob the simmering kettle,
    Songs that seem echoes of "auld lang syne."

And close beside me the cat sits purring,
    Warming her paws at the cheery gleam;
The flames keep flitting, and flicking, and whirring,—
    My mind is lapped in a realm of dream.

—HEINRICH HEINE

A CAT CAME FIDDLING

A cat came fiddling
    Out of a barn,
With a pair of bagpipes
    Under her arm;
She could sing nothing
    But fiddle cum dee,
The mouse has married
    The bumble-bee;
Pipe, cat; dance, mouse:
We'll have a wedding
    At our good house.

—Anonymous

CATS

Fervent suitors and austere scholars
Come in time to love with equal passion
The suave and puissant cats, pride of their homes,
Who, like their masters, bask before the fire.

Friends alike of science and of love,
They search the silent horrors of the night;
Darkness would snatch them for his funeral steeds,
If their stern pride could bend beneath the yoke.

Drowsing, cats take the noble attitude
Of a great sphinx, who, in a desert land,
Sleeps always, dreaming dreams that have no end.

Their fertile loins are full of magic sparks,
And, in the dark profound, like golden sands,
Their burning eyes glow with a mystic fire.

—CHARLES BAUDELAIRE

TO MY CAT

Half loving-kindliness, and half disdain,
    Thou comest to my call serenely suave,
    With humming speech and gracious
        gestures grave,
In salutation courtly and urbane:
Yet must I humble me thy grace to gain—
    For wiles may win thee, but no arts enslave,
    And nowhere gladly thou abidest save
Where naught disturbs the concord of thy reign.

Sphinx of my quiet hearth! who deignst to dwell
    Friend of my toil, companion of mine ease,
    Thine is the lore of Ra and Rameses;

        That men forget dost thou
            remember well,
            Beholden still in blinking
        reveries,
            With somber sea-green
        gaze inscrutable.

—Rosamund Ball Watson

22

3

The Victorian Cat as Predator

"Whence hast thou then, thou witless Puss,
The magic power to charm us thus?
Is it, that in thy glaring eye
And rapid movements we descry
A lion darting on his prey?
A tiger at his ruthless play?"

THE CAT'S CRUELTY

Of all the cruel things there are,
A cat is cruelest by far.
While other creatures kill outright,
To persecute is her delight.

So when you hear that Pussy's prey
Successfully has got away,
You should enthusiastic be,
And ask for strawb'ry jam for tea.

—E. V. LUCAS

PUSSY-CAT, PUSSY-CAT

"Pussy-cat, Pussy-cat,
　　Where have you been?"
"I've been to London,
　　To look at the Queen."
"Pussy-cat, Pussy-cat,
　　What did you do there?"
"I frightened a little mouse
　　Under her chair."

—Anonymous

25

SHE SIGHTS A BIRD

She sights a Bird—she chuckles—
She flattens—then she crawls—
She runs without the look of feet—
Her eyes increase to Balls—

Her Jaws stir—twitching—hungry—
Her Teeth can hardly stand—
She leaps, but Robin leaped the first—
Ah, Pussy, of the Sand,

The Hopes so juicy ripening—
You almost bathed your Tongue—
When Bliss disclosed a hundred Wings—
And fled with every one—

—EMILY DICKINSON

TEN LITTLE MICE

Ten little mice sat down to spin;
Pussy past by, and just looked in:
"What are you at, my jolly ten?"
"We're making coats for gentlemen."

"Shall I come in and cut your threads?"
"No; for, Puss, you'd bite off our heads!"

—Anonymous

The Victorian Cat as Comedian

"Some Cat-land fancies, drawn and dressed
To cheer your mind when it's depressed."

THE GENIAL GRIMALKIN

There was an old cat named Macduff
Who could joke till you cried, "Hold, enough!"
His wife and his child so persistently smiled
That their cheeks got a permanent puff.

—J. G. FRANCIS

A VERY HAPPY FAMILY

The mother sings a song of youth and May,
The father doth the festive fiddle play,
Neighbors strolling on the fence
Stop and smile with joy intense,
While the happy kittens dance the livelong day.

—J. G. FRANCIS

31

A DUTIFUL PARENT

Cried a cat to his wife, "See, my dear,
The superlative circus is here!
With the children we'll go,—'tis our duty, you know,
Their young minds to enlighten and cheer."

—J. G. FRANCIS

A CAT GETS THE LAST LAUGH

—J. G. FRANCIS

THE OWL AND
THE PUSSY-CAT

The Owl and the Pussy-cat went to sea
   In a beautiful pea-green boat,
They took some honey, and plenty of money,
   Wrapped up in a five-pound note.
The Owl looked up to the stars above,
   And sang to a small guitar,
"O lovely Pussy! O Pussy, my love,
   What a beautiful Pussy you are,
      You are,
      You are!
   What a beautiful Pussy you are!"
And hand in hand, on the edge of the sand,
   They danced by the light of the moon,
      The moon,
      The moon,
They danced by the light of the moon.

Pussy said to the Owl, "You elegant fowl!
   How charmingly sweet you sing!
O let us be married! too long we have tarried:

But what shall we do for a ring?"
They sailed away for a year and a day,
    To the land where the Bong-tree grows
And there in a wood a Piggy-wig stood
    With a ring at the end of his nose,
        His nose,
        His nose,
With a ring at the end of his nose.

"Dear Pig, are you willing to sell for one shilling
    Your ring?" Said the Piggy, "I will."
So they took it away, and were married next day
    By the Turkey who lives on the hill.
They dined on mince, and slices of quince,
    Which they ate with a runcible spoon;
And hand in hand, on the edge of the sand,
    They danced by the light of the moon,
        The moon,
        The moon,
They danced by the light of the moon.

—EDWARD LEAR

THE CHESHIRE CAT

As Alice was making her way through Wonderland, she was a little startled by seeing the Cheshire Cat sitting on a bough of a tree a few yards off.

The Cat only grinned when it saw Alice. It looked good-natured, she thought: still it had *very* long claws and a great many teeth, so she felt it ought to be treated with respect.

"Cheshire Puss," she began, rather timidly, as she did not at all know whether it would like the name: however, it only grinned a little wider. "Come, it's pleased so far," thought Alice, and she went on, "Would you tell me, please, which way I ought to walk from here?"

"That depends a good deal on where you want to get to," said the Cat.

"I don't much care where——" said Alice.

"Then it doesn't matter which way you walk," said the Cat.

"——so long as I get *somewhere*," Alice added as an explanation.

"Oh, you're sure to do that," said the Cat, "if you only walk long enough."

Alice felt that this could not be denied, so she tried another question. "What sort of people live about here?"

"In *that* direction," the Cat said, waving its right paw round, "lives a Hatter; and in *that* direction," waving the other paw, "lives a March Hare. Visit either you like: they're both mad."

"But I don't want to go among mad people," Alice remarked.

"Oh, you can't help that," said the Cat: "we're all mad here. I'm mad. You're mad."

"How do you know I'm mad?" said Alice.

"You must be," said the Cat, "or you wouldn't have come here."

Then the Cheshire Cat started to vanish quite slowly, beginning with the end of the tail, and ending with the grin, which remained some time after the rest of it had gone.

"Well! I've often seen a cat without a grin," thought Alice; "but a grin without a cat! It's the most curious thing I ever saw in all my life!"

—LEWIS CARROLL

5

The Victorian Cat as Independent Philosopher

"Talk not to me about your dog,
It is but idle chat;
Give me that calm philosopher
Of hearth and home, the cat."

KIT'S CRADLE
(THE KITTEN SPEAKS)

They've taken the cozy bed away
    That I made myself with the Shetland shawl,
And set me a hamper of scratchy hay,
    By that great black stove in the entrance-hall.

I won't sleep there; I'm resolved on that!
  They may think I will, but they little know
There's a soft persistence about a cat
  That even a little kitten can show.

I wish I knew what to do but pout,
  And spit at the dogs and refuse my tea;
My fur's feeling rough, and I rather doubt
  Whether stolen sausages agree with me.

On the drawing-room sofa they've closed the door,
  They've turned me out of the easy-chairs;
I wonder it never struck me before
  That they make their beds for themselves upstairs.

I've found a crib where they won't find me,
  Though they're crying "Kitty!" all over the house.
Hunt for the slipper! and riddle-my-ree!
  A cat can keep as still as a mouse.

It's rather unwise, perhaps, to purr,
  But they'll never think of the wardrobe-shelves.
I am happy in every hair of my fur;
  They may keep the hamper and hay themselves.

—JULIANA EWING

THE CONTEMPLATIVE LIFE

$\mathcal{F}$ROM the dawn of creation the cat has known his place, and he has kept it, practically untamed and unspoiled by man. He has *retenue*. Of all animals, he alone attains to the Contemplative Life. He regards the wheel of existence from without, like the Buddha. There is no pretense of sympathy about the cat. He lives alone, aloft, sublime, in a wise passiveness. He is excessively proud; and, when he is made the subject of conversation, will cast one glance of scorn, and leave the room in which personalities are bandied. All expressions of emotion he scouts as frivolous and insincere, except, indeed, in the ambrosial night, when, free from the society of mankind, he pours forth his soul in strains of unpremeditated art. The paltry pay and paltry praise of humanity he despises, like Edgar Poe. He does not exhibit the pageant of his bleeding heart; he does not

howl when people die, nor explode in cries of
delight when his master returns from a journey.
With quiet courtesy, he remains in his proper and
comfortable place, only venturing into view when
something he approves of, such as fish or game,
makes its appearance. On the rights of property he
is firm. If a strange cat enters his domain, he is up in
claws to resist invasion. It was for these qualities,
probably, that the cat was worshiped by the ancient
Egyptians.—ANDREW LANG

AN APPRECIATION

I VALUE in the cat the independent and almost
ungrateful spirit which prevents her from
attaching herself to anyone, the indifference with
which she passes from the salon to the housetop.
When we caress her, she stretches herself and
arches her back responsively; but this is because she
feels an agreeable sensation, not because she takes a
silly satisfaction, like the dog, in faithfully loving a
thankless master. The cat lives alone, has no need
of society, obeys only when she pleases, pretends
to sleep that she may see the more clearly, and
scratches everything on which she can lay her paw.
—CHATEAUBRIAND

A CAT

Philosopher and comrade, not for thee
The fond and foolish love which binds the dog;
Only a quiet sympathy which sees
Through all my faults, and bears with them awhile.
Be lenient still, and have some faith in me,
Gentlest of skeptics, sleepiest of friends.

—JULES LEMAITRE

6

The Victorian Cat as the Embodiment of Fear

"The cat—especially the black cat—has often been seen as the virtual embodiment of man's deepest, darkest fears."

THE WITCH CAT

$\mathcal{I}$NNUMERABLE legends cluster around the cat during the picturesque centuries of superstition, when men were poor in letters, but rich in vivid imaginings; when they were densely ignorant, but never dull. Even after the Dark Ages had grown light, there was no lifting of the gloom which enveloped Pussy's pathway, there was no visible soft-ening of her lot. The stories told of her impish wickedness have the same general character through-out Europe. We meet them with modest variations in France, Germany, Sweden, Denmark, England, Scotland, and Wales. It was a belated woodcutter of Brittany who saw with horror-stricken eyes thirteen cats dancing in sacrilegious glee around a wayside crucifix. One he killed with his axe, and the other twelve disappeared in a trice. It was a charcoal-burner in the Black Forest who, hearing strange noises near his kiln at night, arose from bed, and stepped into the clearing. Before him, motionless in the moonlight, sat three cats. He stooped to pick up a stone, and the relic of Saint Gildas he carried in his bosom fell from its snapt string upon the ground. Immediately his arm hung helpless, and he could not touch the stone. Then one of the cats said to its

companions: "For the sake of his wife, who is my gossip, sisters, let him go!" and the next morning he was found lying unconscious, but unharmed, across the forest road.

From Scandinavia, where the fair white cats of Freija were once as honored as were Odin's ravens and Thor's goats, comes the tale of the haunted mill, in which dreadful revelry was heard at night, and which had been twice burned to the ground on Whitsun Eve. The third year, a traveling tailor, pious and brave, offered to keep watch. He chalked a circle on the floor, wrote the Lord's prayer around it, and waited with patience until midnight. Then a troop of cats crept stealthily in, carrying a great pot of pitch which they hung in the fireplace, lighting the logs beneath it. Soon the pitch bubbled and seethed, and the cats, swinging the pot, tried to overturn it. The tailor drove them away; and when one, who seemed to be the leader, sought to pull him gently outside the magic circle, he cut off its paw with his knife. Upon this, they all fled howling into the night; and the next morning the miller saw with joy his mill standing unharmed, and the great wheel turning merrily in the water. But the miller's wife was ill in bed; and, when the tailor bade her goodbye, she gave him her left hand, hiding beneath the bedclothes the right arm's bleeding stump.

There is also a Scandinavian version of the ever famous story which Sir Walter Scott told to Washington Irving, which "Monk" Lewis told to Shelley, and which, in one form or another, we find embodied in the folklore of every land,—the story of the traveller who saw within a ruined abbey a procession of cats, lowering into its grave a little coffin with a crown upon it. Filled with horror, he hastened from the spot; but when he reached his destination, he could not forbear relating to a friend the wonder he had seen. Scarcely had the tale been told, when his friend's cat, who lay curled up tranquilly by the fire, sprang to his feet, cried out, "Then I am the King of the Cats!" and disappeared in a flash up the chimney.—AGNES REPPLIER

THE BLACK CAT

WITH my aversion to my cat, strangely enough, its partiality for myself seemed to increase. It followed my footsteps with a pertinacity which it would be difficult to make the reader comprehend. Whenever I sat, it would crouch beneath my chair, or spring upon my knees, covering me with its loathsome caresses. If I arose to walk it would get between my feet and thus nearly throw me down, or, fastening its long and sharp claws in my dress, clamber, in this manner, to my breast. At such times, although I longed to destroy it with a blow, I was yet withheld from so doing by absolute *dread* of the beast.

Alas! neither by day nor by night knew I the blessing of rest any more! During the former the creature left me no moment alone; and, in the latter, I started, hourly, from dreams of unutterable fear, to find the hot breath of *the thing* upon my face, and its vast weight—an incarnate nightmare that I had no power to shake off—incumbent eternally upon my *heart*!

Beneath the pressure of torments such as these, the feeble remnant of the good within me succumbed. Evil thoughts became my sole intimates— the darkest and most evil of thoughts. The moodiness of my usual temper increased to hatred of all things and of all mankind . . . —EDGAR ALLAN POE

AILUROPHOBIA

𝓜Y RESEARCH brought to me indisputable evidence concerning the large number of people in whom the presence of a cat gives rise to a variety of symptoms. In such persons, the feeling caused by seeing a cat is instantaneous. In the asthma victims, it is slower and cumulative, and may not be felt at all for twenty minutes or more. Certain persons, on seeing a cat, have other symptoms, with or without oppression of breathing.

There may be only fear, terror, disgust. There may be added chilly sensations, horripilation, weakness, locked jaw, or, as in one case, fixed open jaw, rigidity of arms, pallor, nausea, rarely vomiting, pronounced hysterical convulsions, and even temporary blindness. These pass away with removal of the cat, but in a few examples leave the sufferer nervously disturbed for a day. Two report themselves as apt to have dreams of cats, what one of them calls "cat mares."

Five persons, three being women, are alarmed in the presence of the greater cats, caged tigers or lions. A soldier of distinction, much given when younger to tiger hunting, is undisturbed by these great felines, but terrified by the tame cat.

On a study of those who, at sight of cats, have fear, horror, and, in varying degrees, emotional disturbances and distinct physical symptoms, and those whom unseen cats affect, we observe that the same symptomatic expressions attend both groups.

In the first set, sight of the cat informs. Then there are fear, horror, disgust, and more or less of the nervous symptoms already described. In the second set, those who are conscious of unseen cats, some sense, other than sight or hearing, gives the information, and then the symptoms are much the same as when the cat is seen.—S. WEIR MITCHELL, M. D.

7

The Victorian Cat Among the Angels

"If heaven exists for cats above,
All the feline angels call you there with love."

ON THE DEATH OF A CAT, A FRIEND OF MINE, AGED TEN YEARS AND A HALF

Who shall tell the lady's grief
    When her Cat was past relief?
Who shall number the hot tears
    Shed o'er her, belov'd for years?
Who shall say the dark dismay
    Which her dying caused that day?

Come, ye Muses, one and all,
    Come obedient to my call.
Come and mourn, with tuneful breath,
    Each one for a separate death;
And while you in numbers sigh,
    I will sing her elegy.

Of a noble race she came,
    And Grimalkin was her name.
Young and old full many a mouse
    Felt the prowess of her house;
Weak and strong full many a rat
    Cowered beneath her crushing pat;
And the birds around the place
    Shrank from her too close embrace.
But one night, reft of her strength,
    She laid down and died at length.

Lay a kitten by her side,
    In whose life the mother died.
Spare her line and lineage,
    Guard her kitten's tender age,
And that kitten's name as wide
    Shall be known as hers that died.

And whoever passes by
    The poor grave where Puss doth lie,
Softly, softly let him tread,
    Nor disturb her narrow bed.

—CHRISTINA ROSSETTI

LAMENT FOR A BRAVE TABBY

And art thou fallen, and lowly laid,
The housewife's boast, the cellar's aid,
    Great mouser of thy day!
Whose rolling eyes, and aspect dread
Whole whiskered legions oft have fled
    In midnight battle fray.
There breathes no kitten of thy line
But would have given his life for thine.

So thou, remote from pain and strife,
Now reap'st the meed of virtuous life
    In some Elysian grove,
Where endless streams of milk abound,
And soft valerian paints the ground
    Thy joyous footsteps rove;
With Tasso's cat by poems named,
And Whittington's, in story famed,
    Rest blessed, dear cat, in peace.

—ROSAMUND BALL WATSON

FELINE REINCARNATIONS

I sometimes think the pussy-willows gray
Are angel kittens who have lost their way,
    And every bulrush on the river bank
A cat-tail from some lovely cat astray.

Sometimes I think perchance that Allah may,
When he created cats, have thrown away
    The tails he marred in making, and they grew
To cat-tails and to pussy-willows gray.

—OLIVER HERFORD